Learning To Fl

Written and Illustrated by Jamie Reynolds

www.cartoonstrips.com

(optional ramblings)

The content of this book you are holding is pretty much the same as it was in the homemade prototypes I produced back in the early 1990's. One exception is that the art was originally done as a full page frame around text; I reduced each page in a copier and bound the book together in my basement, joined it with a cover (that I screen printed) and had the edges trimmed. I made a bunch of them and sent them all over the place.

Because of the way books are done now, at least this book, the old art had to be chopped and placed in with the text. If you would like to see the original book and the way it was laid out, you should always be able to find a link to the complete book, in webpage form; on my cartoonstrips.com website, if not email me and I'll send you the link.

Some of the jokes are dated; you may not know what "Billy Chips" and "Yard Shadows" are, but I decided not to change much from the original as I wanted to keep it as close to the way it was written while I was an excited student pilot in 1992-1993 – I hope you understand and enjoy.

(more optional ramblings)

I have had a lot of constructive criticism by aviators as well as those good with writing techniques (which I welcomed and still welcome) and I did fix a lot of problems; but you may still find an occasional error in my writing technique and I'm sure not everyone will agree on training methods for student pilots, but, please take this as my nearly 20 year ago attempt to share my passion and excitement as I became a new pilot.

Learning To Fly

Written and Illustrated by Lonnie Reynolds

www.cartoontips.com

(optional ramblings)

The content of this book would be holding up pretty much the same as it was in the homemade prototypes I produced back in the early 1990's. The exception is that the original writing/ drawings in full page frame sound text. I reduced such that then carrier and bound the book together in my basement, glued it with a cover that I screen printed and put the edges trimmed. I made a bunch of them and sent them all over the place.

Because of the way books are done now, at last, this book, the old art had to be chopped and placed in with the text. If you would like to see the original book and the way it was laid out, you should always be able to find a link to the complete book in webpage form on my cartoontips.com website. If I ever remember and I'll keep you the link.

Some of the jokes are dated, you may not know what Sky Chimps are and Skelators but I decided not to change much from the original as I wanted to keep it as close to the way it was back then while I was an excited student pilot in 1994-1995. I hope you understand and enjoy.

(more optional ramblings)

I have had a lot of constructive criticism by aviators as well as those good with writing techniques (which I welcomed and still welcome) and I did fix a lot of problems but you may still find an occasional error in my writing technique and I'm sure not everyone will agree on training methods for student pilots but, please take this as my nearly 20 year old attempt to share my passion and excitement as I became a new pilot.

2

Endorsements and name dropping.

Chuck Yeager gave an endorsement by signing the cover of a book that I sent him to look over, which he did before signing and sending it back. Chuck Yeager is an amazing person – everyone should read **YEAGER: an Autobiography.**

Two time Space Shuttle Pilot and two time Space Shuttle Commander **Tom Henricks** told me back in 1995 that when he retires from NASA, he would gladly write an endorsement for this book. Colonel Henricks did retire, but I decided not to bother him about this, I had already bugged him enough (thanks Tom).

Thanks also to the people at **Aviation Supplies and Academics (ASA)** who liked the book and **almost** published it. I really do appreciate your original interest in the project. (is that contract ready yet Fred?).

This space is reserved for endorsements from **Harrison Ford** and **John Travolta,** my favorite celebrity pilots, – I tried everything to get a copy of this book to these guys and never even came close. But for all my efforts, postage and the disappointments of the books being returned "undeliverable", I decided to dedicate this 12 square inches to that effort.

Finally, I wanted to mention what a good experience I had obtaining a forward for this book from **Paul Poberezny**; Founder of the Experimental Aviation Association. His hand written letters and official correspondence were top notch. Looking over all of our communications from around 1995 I could see how Paul's professionalism and passion for aviation enabled him to start the EAA from one small group of pilots and turn it into the highly respected, worldwide organization it is today.

..here is the letter from Paul with the forward...

Experimental Aircraft Association

Paul H. Poberezny
Founder
Chairman of the Board

James M. Reynolds
532 Lawndale Avenue
Bryan, OH 43506

Dear James:

I found your book to be a very simple, easy to understand publication that would be excellent for the novice. In fact, it would be much like what they would hear from the flight instructors during those hours prior to solo.

At the start of World War II, I was 19-1/2 years of age and giving flight instruction. I had accumulated 275 hours in all sorts of old airplanes, from Cubs to Waco 10's, American Eagles and several homebuilts. When the great need for flight instructors came forth, I had the opportunity to teach Primary flight instruction for 2200 hours at Helena Aero Tech in PT-19's and PT-23's. When I look back, I could not believe that I was actually being paid to fly. All of my aviation cadets graduated from Primary, Basic and Advanced. I even took several dropouts from other classes and they, too, went on to graduate and earn their wings.

Today's flight instructors are operating aircraft of a different breed. The aerodynamics call for little use of the rudder, but the rudder certainly is there and is needed more than many modern day pilots realize.

I would certainly recommend your publication as a starting point for those who desire to enjoy this vast ocean of air above us.

Sincerely,

EXPERIMENTAL AIRCRAFT ASSOCIATION

Paul H. Poberezny
Chairman of the Board

..one of my old table of "continents" and other important stuff pages.

... a bit newer **table of contents**.

Chapter One – The First Lesson...page 9

Chapter Two – Engine Failure?...page 43

Chapter Three – More Lessons...page 51

Chapter Four – Going Solo...page 69

Chapter Five – The Cross Countries...page 77

Chapter Six – Final Preparations and The Flight Test..............page 99

Chapter 1
The First Lesson

"I don't want to be late," Matt thought to himself as he drove speedily towards the airport.

An airplane flew overhead catching his attention. Matt stuck his head out of the window to get a better view of the overtaking aircraft.

"Hey!" Matt grabbed for his hat as the wind caught it and sent it tumbling end over end into the road behind him.

Luckily, after only getting run over by half the wheels of an eighteen wheeler, the hat just needed to be scraped off the pavement and dusted before being placed back onto his head. Matt then hopped back into his car and headed for his first flying lesson.

Matt had always wanted to learn how to fly, at least as long as he could remember. In High School, when all the other guys were taking their dates to movies and dances, Matt would take his date to busy airports and park at the end of the runway so they could watch airplanes. (He never had too many repeat dates.) Matt was then voted "Most likely to be hit by an Airbus" by the girls in his class.

The airport sign appeared over the next hill and Matt would soon be in the air. Thinking about that gave him butterflies as he pulled into the driveway.

"What a beautiful day!" Fred commented aloud over the engine noise of the small Cessna. "It doesn't get much nicer than this!" Fred could see the skyline of Catalina and that was almost 45 miles away. It really was a clear day.

The first flight of the morning usually belonged to him. Warming up the airplane before any of his students arrived was his duty. "Somebody had to do it," Fred told himself.

Of course, Fred was just making an excuse to go flying. He couldn't get enough of it. Today, Fred circled town 3 or 4 times and watched people go to work and to school. Cars were filling up the parking lot at the Mini-Mall, (they were having a sale today). A lot of people were stopping at Waffle-Burger for a quick bite. As Fred flew over the road that led to the airport he saw somebody lose their hat out of their car window.

Looking at his watch Fred saw that it was time to get back; Matt should be arriving at the airport soon. He reached down for the throttle knob and reduced the power. The airplane started to descend as Fred turned towards the airport. He positioned himself for a landing on runway 36.

A few airplanes were parked here and there and some birds were racing around the hangers. The only other movement was the windsock doing a slow dance in the breeze.

Matt was peeking into a hanger when suddenly he heard the hum of an aircraft. It must have been the plane he had seen earlier.

Matt waved as the small airplane flew overhead. The pilot saw him wave and rocked the wings. That surprised Matt, he hadn't expected a response.

The airplane touched down onto the runway with its rear wheels first leaving the nose wheel to fall slowly to the pavement. It was a beautiful landing. After slowing down, the plane turned off of the runway and headed for the hangers.

Matt decided against standing right there as the plane taxied in. He quickly stepped behind a fence to be sure that he was out of the way.

Fred opened the window letting the springtime air circulate inside the cockpit. "That was a good flight," he thought to himself as he taxied off the runway, "this will be a great day to give lessons."

Reaching down to a lever on the instrument panel, Fred retracted the wing flaps while he taxied. He then switched off the carburetor heat letting the engine run noticeably smoother.

After parking the airplane in front of one of the hangers, Fred switched off the beacon light and radios then killed the engine. The propeller spun to a stop.

The airport was once again quiet, with only the birds breaking the silence.

Fred turned off the ignition switch and then the master switch, got himself un-belted from the seat and stepped out of the plane. He then went over to introduce himself to Matt.

"Hello, you must be Matt. I'm Fred; I'll be your instructor."

Matt shook his hand, "is this the plane that we'll be flying?" Matt asked.

"Good ol' Delta Bravo, yes, this is her. Isn't she a beauty?" Fred kicked a tire with affection. "Here, let me show you how to pre-flight an airplane."

Fred explained how important it is to inspect the airplane thoroughly before every flight.

Fred handed Matt the checklist used for the pre-flight. "There sure are a lot of things to check," Matt said.

"It really only takes a short time to do properly," Fred explained, "It's important that every pilot pre-flights their aircraft."

The first thing they did was check the actual fuel quantity by measuring the depth of the fuel in each tank. "We don't trust fuel gauges in airplanes as much as we trust them in cars." Fred replaced the fuel cap and stepped down off the stool. "Fuel gauges are only required to be accurate when your tanks are empty."

"Wow!" Matt exclaimed, "that's like my old broken watch, it's only right twice a day."

"When we know how many gallons of fuel we have on board," Fred began, "we can figure how many hours we can stay in the air. Miles per gallon does not concern us nearly as much as hours per gallon."

"Why is that?" Matt asked.

"Let's say that we fly at 100 miles an hour," Fred began, "if we fly against a headwind of 30 miles an hour, that would drop our speed over the ground to 70."

"It's like swimming upstream," Matt commented.

Fred nodded, "but if you turned and flew directly downwind," Fred continued, "you would really cover some ground, you would add the speed of the wind to the speed of the airplane."

They went all around the airplane, they checked everything. "Why don't you hop into the left seat," Fred said as he opened the door for him. "The pilot sits on the left; I'll be your co-pilot so I'll sit on the right."

"It's a good thing there are two steering wheels," Matt began, "I don't feel like much of a pilot yet."

Fred climbed into the right seat. "Lesson one," Fred smiled, "these are the yokes, not steering wheels, as you will soon see."

Fred told Matt how to adjust his seat so that he could reach the pedals on the floor.

Matt looked at the pedals on the floor. "Are these the gas and the brakes?" he asked.

"By pushing the tops of those pedals we do activate the brakes," Fred began, "but the rudder pedal's main function is the control the rudder back there on the tail, and the steerable nose wheel..."

"We steer with our feet?" Matt sounded surprised.

"When we taxi we steer with our feet," Fred continued, "it takes a bit of getting used to but you'll get the hang of it."

"Pushing in the throttle brings in full engine power and pulling it out reduces the power." Fred explained as he worked the knob on the instrument panel.

"What does the yoke do?" Matt asked as he moved the wheel in front of him.

"The yoke has two functions," Fred began. "Moving the yoke in and out raises and lowers the elevator." Fred pointed behind him at the tail. "And turning the yoke right and left controls the ailerons out there on the wings," Fred turned the wheel a few times.

"When one aileron moves up," Matt pointed at the left wing, "the other aileron moves down," Matt looked out at the right wing.

"The wing with the lowered aileron is forced up and the wing with the raised aileron is forced down," Fred explained. "The plane will bank in the direction that the wheel is turned." Fred's hand illustrated a left bank.

Matt thought for a moment, "So we turn the plane with ailerons."

Fred smiled, "a bank is only one of the things necessary for a turn." Fred opened the glovebox, pulled out a checklist and handed it to Matt, "let's get the engine started. It will be much easier to demonstrate that in the air." Once again the silence of the morning was broken when the engine roared to life.

Fred gave Matt a quick demonstration on how to taxi. He then instructed Matt to take them out to the end of the runway.

"I keep wanting to steer with the yoke," Matt shouted with excitement, "but it doesn't do anything."

Fred laughed a little and replied, "Steering with your feet takes a while to get used to." Fred reached down to shut off the cabin heat; the sun's warmth was taking the chill out of the air.

It was very easy to over correct, Matt thought to himself as he tried desperately to track the centerline of the taxiway.

The airplane weaved back and forth until it reached an intersection.

"Which way should I turn?" Matt asked noticing that there were taxiways going off in both directions.

"Well, we always want to take-off and land into the wind," Fred began, "now, which way is the wind coming from?"

Matt opened the window and put his hand outside, "from the propeller."

Fred grinned as he shook his head, "that is true, but the wind we're concerned with right now is out of the north," he pointed at the wind sock.

"So we want to go to the south end of the runway," Matt stated.

Fred nodded his head in approval, "very good Matt, take me to the south end of the runway."

The airplane turned right onto the taxiway that led to the south end of the runway and continued on, weaving back and forth all the way.

Fred directed Matt not to taxi onto the runway yet. "We have to do a few more things before we take-off; we use a checklist to help us remember those things." Fred flipped over the checklist in his hand.

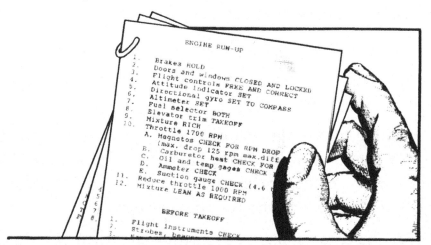

ENGINE RUN-UP
1. Brakes HOLD
2. Doors and windows CLOSED AND LOCKED
3. Flight controls FREE AND CORRECT
4. Attitude Indicator SET
5. Directional gyro SET TO COMPASS
6. Altimeter SET
7. Fuel selector BOTH
8. Elevator trim TAKEOFF
9. Mixture RICH
10. Throttle 1700 RPM
    A. Magnetos CHECK FOR RPM DROP
       (max. drop 125 rpm max.diff
    B. Carburetor heat CHECK FOR
    C. Oil and temp gages CHECK
    D. Ammeter CHECK
    E. Suction gauge CHECK (4.6
11. Reduce throttle 1000 RPM
12. Mixture LEAN AS REQUIRED

BEFORE TAKEOFF
1. Flight instruments CHECK
2. Strobes, beaco

One of the first things the list said to do was to make sure that their doors and windows were secure. "We also need to check that our seats are latched properly," Fred added.

Matt wiggled back and forth a few times.

"It's really important," Fred explained, "when we climb, it's like going up a steep hill, if your seat's not locked..."

"I'll end up in the back of the plane," Matt finished.

"Yes," Fred agreed, "and flying is exciting enough without that happening."

Checking the flight controls to make sure that they move freely and in the correct direction; was the next thing on the list.

"When we turn the yoke all the way to the left, the left aileron should be up," Fred pointed out at the left wing, "and at the same time, the right aileron should be down," he pointed at the other wing. Fred then turned the wheel to verify that the opposite was true.

Next, he had Matt pull out on the yoke. When he did this, the elevator back on the tail moved up.

"And when you push the yoke in, the elevator will go down," Fred explained, "we also check that the rudder pedals are moving the rudder in the proper direction too." Fred worked the rudder pedals and pointed behind him, "What does the checklist say to do next?"

"Looks like we have to set the instruments," replied Matt.

Fred showed Matt the three instruments that they needed to set before take-off.

"Your heading indicator tells you what direction you are going, it needs to be set to the compass." Fred dialed in the proper heading. "The heading indicator will give you an accurate reading even while the plane is turning, climbing or descending, where the compass will not."

"The attitude indicator shows your relationship with the horizon," Fred continued, "degree of bank, climbs or descents..."

Matt pointed at the instrument, "there's a little airplane on the dial."

"Yeah, that represents you, that bar behind it represents the horizon," Fred replied. "And finally, the altimeter shows us our height above sea level..."

"What good is that? We're a thousand miles from the sea," stated Matt.

Fred smiled as he leaned back in the seat, "we'll save that explanation for ground school."

Fred increased the throttle to 1700 RPM. He then showed Matt how to check that both magnetos were working properly.

"Unlike a car, an airplane has two spark plugs per cylinder," Fred spoke loudly over the engine noise, "in fact it has two ignition systems. If one fails, the engine will remain running; that is why we check both systems before flight."

Fred then showed Matt the carburetor heat knob. "We should get a slight RPM drop when we pull out the carburetor heat."

"What is that for?" Matt asked.

22

"Air cools when it is forced through the venturi of the carburetor," Fred explained, "cold air can't hold as much moisture as warm air so that moisture is squeezed out. Ice can form inside the carburetor even in 70 degree weather. Applying "carb" heat moves warm air through the carburetor melting that ice."

They checked the engine gauges and reduced the throttle back to a hum, "we need to make a radio call and then we can take-off," Fred handed Matt the mike.

"The thing I worried about the most when I started taking flying lessons was using the radio properly," Fred confessed, "I thought I'd go all fumble-mouthed and not know what to say, but, it's really quite simple. All we have to do is tell other air-traffic in the area **who** we are, **where** we are and **what** we want to do." Matt keyed the mike, "HELLO MY NAME IS MATT AND I'M IN AN AIRPLANE..."

Fred reached over and took the mike from Matt, "I like your enthusiasm, but I really should give you an example first; "SUMMIT COUNTY TRAFFIC, CESSNA 543 DELTA BRAVO DEPARTING RUNWAY 36." Fred looked for traffic again before taxiing onto the runway.

The engine went to full throttle; Matt felt himself being pushed deeper into his seat from the acceleration. Faster and faster they went, the pavement underneath them was starting to blur. Matt wondered how fast they needed to go before they would take-off. They were 20 feet off the runway before he could finish that thought.

It was incredible! In only a few moments they went from not being able to see past the tree line to having an extraordinary view for miles and miles. Houses, fields, factories... the whole town was on display out of the window.

Matt could see Main Street, the school, all of downtown. He spotted the Waffle-Burger that he had planned to stop at on his way home; Matt loved their sticky buns.

He could see kids playing ball in the park, people walking in and out of Kay's Mart. There was a fellow working on a roof, fixing some shingles or something. He was waving his arms about in the air with great enthusiasm, Matt figured that he must be waving up at them, he must really like airplanes. Matt waved back.

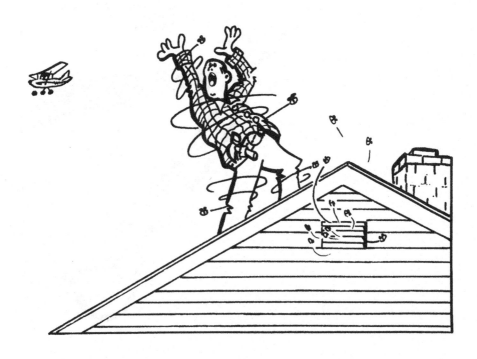

Fred kept quiet. He noticed that Matt's attention was focused on the view outside. He would give Matt a few minutes before he started to demonstrate the effects of the controls.

Fred knew what it felt like. He would spend hours watching the town below him whenever he got hired to tow a banner around. There were always plenty of things to watch. It gave you a powerful feeling to know that almost everyone was looking up at you, especially if you were towing a banner.

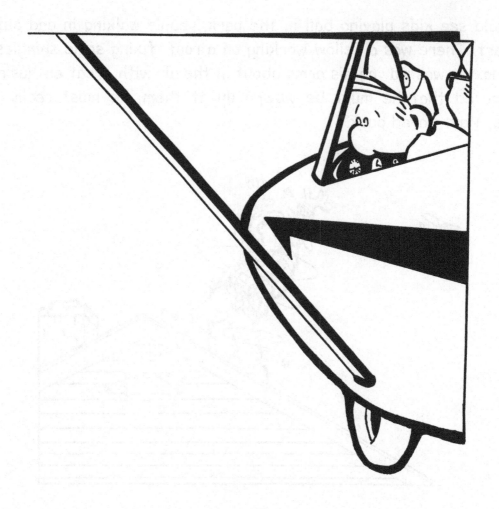

Matt finally managed to take his eyes off of the scenery. "Fred, I definitely want to learn how to fly!"

"I was hoping that you would say that," Fred replied. He leveled the plane off at 2500 feet; added trim then took his hands off the yoke, "look Matt, no hands."

"Wow, autopilot!" Matt announced.

"This plane doesn't have autopilot," Fred explained, "but it is stable, you don't have to fight to control it."

"So how do you make the airplane do what you want to do?" Matt asked.

Fred grinned, "That depends on what you want to do. Let's say we want to go up..."

"Use the up elevator," Matt said proudly.

Fred looked over at him, "okay Matt, let's see if you are right. Using the elevator, take us up to 3000 feet." He said as he pointed at the altimeter.

Matt pulled back slowly on the yoke. He smiled confidently as they started to gain altitude.

Fred smiled when he saw the airspeed dropping.

Matt's smile changed to a confused frown when; after gaining barely a hundred feet, the plane would climb no more. The more he tried to climb, the steeper the nose of the airplane would point into the sky, and the airspeed was falling fast.

Matt started to give up.

"Don't give up yet," Fred said as he took over the controls. The nose continued to point higher and higher as Fred pulled back even further on the wheel.

All Matt could see out of the windshield was blue sky. Suddenly a warning buzzer sounded. Fred continued pulling back on the elevator. The plane seemed to hang there for a moment;

...Fred pulled the yoke out just a little bit more...

"Eeeep..." Matt gasped when the bottom dropped out. The nose of the airplane was now pointing toward the earth below.

"Release back pressure, full throttle, carb heat in, nose up, positive rate of climb." Fred looked over at Matt and smiled, "Now that we're back where we started from," he pointed at the altimeter, "I'll show you how to gain altitude and keep it."

"What happened?" Matt asked.

"That was a stall," Fred explained, "the airplane just couldn't continue flying at that speed, so it stopped flying. When the nose dropped, the airspeed increased until we were flying again. We normally wouldn't get into stalls on the first lesson, but you sort of asked for it; the elevator is not the up and down control."

Fred pointed the nose of the airplane up above the horizon slightly causing the airspeed to decrease. He then added power allowing the plane to continue its climb without losing any more airspeed.

"What makes an airplane go up?" Matt asked.

"Lift is generated when the wing moves through the air," Fred explained, "if the wing develops more lift than the airplane weighs, the plane will go up."

Matt nodded; that part made sense anyway, "but how do you control the lift?"

"You can move the wing faster through the air," Fred began, "which requires throttle. Or, you can increase the angle at which the oncoming wind strikes the wing; the elevator will change that angle..."

"Ah ha!" Matt pointed an accusing finger at Fred, "You said the elevator is not the up and down control."

Fred grinned, "the elevator lets us change the angle that the wing meets the oncoming air," he put his finger up as to make a point, "the power from the engine is the only thing in the world that will let us keep that excess lift without losing airspeed."

"Like we did before," Matt said.

"Yes, like we did before," Fred agreed.

Reaching 3000 feet, Fred leveled the nose against the horizon. Then he allowed the airspeed to come up some before pulling the throttle back to cruise power. "If the throttle is the up and down control," Fred began, "then what control will we use to go down?"

Matt pointed at the throttle knob.

"Good," Fred commended Matt.

"It's like riding a bicycle," Matt stated.

Fred looked over at Matt and asked, "How so?"

Matt replied, "If you're riding along and the road starts sloping downward, you don't need to pedal as hard."

"You can just glide down that hill," Fred interrupted as he made a swooping motion with his hand.

"But as soon as you start up the next hill your speed drops fast," Matt continued, "If you don't start pedaling real hard, your bike will stop."

"It could fall over too," Fred said recalling the time his pant leg got caught in the sprocket of his Schwinn Stingray. He was halfway up Mammoth Hill when his bell-bottom decided it liked the comfort and security of being pinched between sprocket and chain. Fred had managed an uncoordinated hop onto the grassy shoulder than over he went, end over end. He tumbled down Mammoth Hill with the Schwinn attached to his leg. Fred wondered if anybody else ever had the unique feeling that only hundreds of pine needles in your shorts can give you.

After guiding Matt through a few more climbs and descents, Fred figured it was time to introduce Matt to the wonderful world of turns.

"Take us back down to 2500 feet," Fred instructed, "and we'll move on to something else."

Matt reduced the power and the nose dropped slightly below the horizon line. The airplane started a gradual descent.

Matt looked over and saw Fred looking out the window at some scenery. He could tell Fred was smiling. It made Matt feel good to know that Fred was pleased with him so far.

After leveling out at 2500 feet Matt waited for instructions from Fred.

"Let's do some turns, help me look for other traffic." Fred told Matt how they should always look for traffic before any maneuver. "Would you like to see a tight fast turn, or a wide slow turn?"

Matt replied, "The tight turn sounds like fun."

After checking the area for any other aircraft, Fred went into a steep turn.

Fred pushed in the rudder while banking the airplane. At 50 degrees of bank he released some aileron and rudder pressures and fed in up elevator to hold their altitude. The world pivoted around their left wingtip.

Matt got scrunched in his seat a little bit and his arms felt heavy. It was an exhilarating feeling. All he could do was look out the window at the ground below. "This is great!" Matt yelled, "It feels like we are sideways."

"Not quite. Almost though... isn't this fun?" After completing one left turn Fred pushed in on the right rudder pedal as he rolled in right aileron, then added some positive elevator pressure and went directly into a steep right turn. Fred told Matt to follow along on the controls as they did some more turns. "This hands on experience will help you understand chapter two in your flight training manual."

There were a few houses scattered here and there below them. Matt could see activity in some of the yards. "Those people on the ground must think that we're nuts!" He shouted as he tried to wave at them.

"Hey Harold, do you see that air-o-plane up there?" said the lady in the flowered dress to her husband, "it looks like it's chasing its tail."

Harold got up from his garden, wiped the perspiration off his brow and stared at the plane for a while, "near as I can figure... they must be lost." He deduced then returned to his daisies.

The lady in the flowered dress muttered something about darn fools then turned to her husband and said, "Well I'd hate to be up there. It just isn't natural. Flying is for the birds. Even birds can't get it right, the way they go banging into my picture window all the time." She turned to go back into the house. "I'm gonna keep my feet right here on the ground and do important things like the Good Lord intended."

She looked at her watch. "Are you coming in? "Mayberry" will be on television in 15 minutes."

"WOW! COOL! That's what I want I wanna be; A PILOT! I'm going to be a pilot when I grow up." Billy stated while running around the yard with his arms spread and making a buzzing noise with his lips.

Billy's Sister Darla looked away from the circling airplane for a moment and said, "I thought you wanted to be a baseball player?"

"Old news Darla, that was yesterday." Billy explained. "Baseball players can get hurt and that might end a career. I'd be on the road for weeks. Why should I risk getting a bad sunburn or hit by a pitch?"

"Because when you're old enough to play in the Majors, you'll make a million dollars a game, that's why."

Billy thought for a moment about what Darla had said. Then he took another look up at the circling airplane. Turning to his sister he said, "Hey Darla, do you wanna play catch?"

Matt was starting to understand the mechanical inputs necessary for a proper turn, but didn't yet understand the reasons behind them. Fred told him not to worry, that it would all make sense with ground study and more practice.

"Right rudder and right aileron at the same time," Matt spoke as the airplane banked to the right.

"The ailerons roll the airplane into a turn," Fred explained, "the rudder is needed to correct for something called adverse yaw."

Matt centered the ailerons and rudder. The plane stayed in the bank turn.

"When we use the ailerons," Fred continued on, "the raised outside wing has more drag because it has more lift. This makes it want to slow down and drag the nose to the outside of the turn." Fred tried to illustrate this with his hand, "using rudder in the same direction of the turn keeps the nose of the airplane aligned with the direction of travel."

Matt noticed that they were losing altitude.

"The reason that we use up elevator during a turn," Fred pulled out on the yoke slightly, "is because some of the lift that was supporting our weight is now being used to pull the airplane through the turn. That doesn't leave enough lift to hold our altitude. Using the correct amount of elevator gives us the lift we need to hold our altitude."

Fred looked at his watch, "Okay Matt, take me back to the airport."

"Matt looked around. He then turned the airplane and looked around some more. He had no idea of where they were. The fields below went on forever, the roads criss-crossed every which way. He could see three towns from here, "which one was Summit?" Matt was stumped, "I think I'm lost," he said admitting defeat.

"Nonsense," Fred replied, "Which direction did we fly away from the airport?"

Matt thought for a moment, remembering that they had flown over the center of town; he answered, "West."

"And what did we do?" Fred asked.

"We flew west for quite a while practicing climbs and descents, and then we just went around in circles." Matt had figured it out now, "the airport should be to our east." Matt pointed out the right window.

Fred smiled as he pointed out the left window, "your other east."

"There are several ways to avoid getting lost Matt," Fred pulled a map out of the glove box. "The main method is with an aeronautical chart." Fred unfolded a portion of the chart and pointed out Summit City. "Roads, rivers and anything else that is visible from the air can be shown on the chart. Look, over there is Lake Nofishinit." First Fred pointed out the window at the lake in the distance and then at the lake depicted on the chart.

Matt stared a moment a Lake Nofishinit. He could just barely pick out the camping area where he and his dad pitch a tent a couple times a year. "This year we are going to bring hotdogs," Matt thought to himself remembering that they hadn't ever caught a fish in that stupid lake.

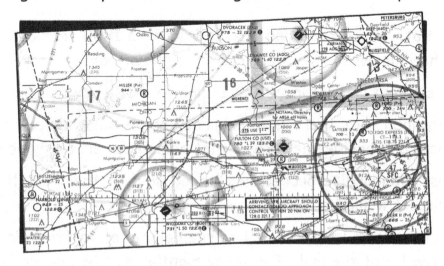

"At this point we should make a radio call to the airport." Fred began, "we need to get wind and runway conditions, traffic information and anything else that might affect our flight in."

Matt made a call with Fred's help; "SUMMIT COUNTY CESSNA 543 DELTA BRAVO, 5 MILES WEST REQUEST AIRPORT ADVISORY."

The reply came back before Matt hung up the microphone.

"3 DELTA BRAVO, SUMMIT COUNTY WINDS ARE STEADY FROM THE NORTH AT 8 KNOTS, FAVORING RUNWAY 36, NO OTHER TRAFFIC REPORTED."

"3 DELTA BRAVO." Fred acknowledged the transmission. "We can shorten "543 DELTA BRAVO" TO "3 DELTA BRAVO" after our first call up."

Matt hadn't really noticed the shortened version but was glad that Fred had explained it anyway.

"We had better descend to traffic pattern altitude." Fred announced. "Do you remember how?"

"What's a traffic pattern?" Matt asked.

Fred's expression turned into a "Oh yeah, I guess he wouldn't know that" look.

He told Matt to go ahead and descend down to 1800 feet and level off, he would show him when they were closer to the airport.

Matt leveled out and returned the engine to cruise power.

Fred explained that there is a imaginary rectangular shaped pattern in the sky above and beside the runway that helps keep order in the sky.

"We must standardize procedures," Fred said. "Otherwise, the traffic above an airport would be chaos."

Matt could understand that. He had seen plenty of traffic related chaos in the parking lot of the mall. The three months that he had worked at the

Coffee-Hut drive thru had earned him a silver spoon; for bravery. The way those cars go through there. It's a good thing they have concrete bumpers around those little buildings.

Fred made another call, "CESSNA 3 DELTA BRAVO, DOWNWIND FOR RUNWAY 36."

The downwind leg of the traffic pattern is parallel to the runway but in the opposite direction from which they will be landing.

"Time to add carburetor heat and reduce the throttle," Fred worked the two knobs in the center of the instrument panel, "let's get this airplane on the ground."

"We need to get the airplane slowed down," Fred stated, "from a hundred miles an hour down to around 70. We will hold that airspeed to within a few feet above the runway."

The left rudder pedal sunk from below Matt's foot at the same time a Fred rolled in aileron. "We're turning onto the base leg of the traffic pattern. We need to look for traffic, reduce the power and then add some flaps, any planes on your side Matt?"

Matt looked out into the distance, "I don't see any, what are flaps?"

"I'll show you in a moment," Fred replied as he turned the airplane towards the runway, "for now I'll just say that the flaps help us get down."

Fred pulled the throttle knob to idle and pointed out to Matt that they were a little high up.

It felt like he had applied the brakes. When Fred moved that flap lever Matt would have bet the airplane had just slowed down.

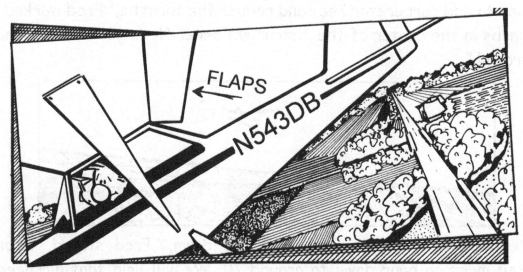

"We haven't slowed down," Fred said as he pushed forward on the elevator, "I know it may have felt like we did, but we didn't. If I were to let the nose of the airplane rise up now like it wants to," he continued, "we would slow down. We would slow down too fast. To prevent that I need to increase the angle that we are descending to keep our airspeed up."

He explained to Matt that flaps create a lot of drag. Like a parachute slowing down a falling object, flaps on the wings of an airplane enable it to come in for a landing at a much steeper angle without building up excess airspeed. It is the change of descent angles that makes it feel like you slowed down.

The wheels touched down gently onto the surface of the runway. Matt had survived his first flying lesson.

Fred retracted the flaps, pushed in the carb heat and leaned the mixture slightly. "Why don't you taxi us back to the hanger Matt?"

"3 DELTA BRAVO, WILL YOU BE REQUIRING FUEL TODAY, OR ARE YOU JUST VISITING?"

Fred grinned, "She knows darn well..." he picked up the mike and replied, "NEGATIVE SUMMIT UNICOM, I WORK HERE. MY NAME IS FRED."

The woman's voice came back over the radio, "FRED HUH, COULD YOU SPELL THAT?" you could tell that she busted out laughing before the mike clicked off.

Fred shook his head, "that is a good example of how not to use the radio Matt; we could get into trouble for doing stuff like that."

"You could get both the F.A.A. and the F.C.C. on your case." Matt added.

Fred's eyes widened at the thought, "and we definitely don't want that to happen." He helped Matt handle the sharp turn by the hanger. "Let's park it here."

They pulled out the checklist and went over the shutdown procedure before turning off the engine. After the propeller stopped spinning the airport was quiet once more.

"Now what had gotten into you?" bellowed Fred humorously as he walked into the office.

A pleasant woman sat at a desk facing them. "I'm sorry Fred. I know I shouldn't do that. But, I'm in such a good mood. It's such a beautiful day. The spring air is getting to me and I ate too many donuts."

Fred looked over at his almost empty box of double-frosted, twice filled, sugar coated Bon Bombs. "What happened to my donuts?" he asked politely.

"I had to eat them. They were trying to escape." She explained, "one of them even took you bag of Fritos as a hostage."

Fred shot a glance over to his lunch bag, it was opened. "I give up," he said as he flopped into a chair.

"That's just what the Fritos said." She turned around to face Matt, "Hello, I'm Kristen. You must be Matt. How was your first lesson?" she said as she offered her hand.

He shook Kristen's hand and said, "Oh, we had a great lesson. It was the most exciting thing I've ever done."

"Well good," she replied, "and I bet you learned something too."

Matt nodded, he had learned a lot. In fact it felt like all that he had learned was tangled in a big jumbled knot between his ears. He would have to go home, relax and go over what he had learned slowly.

Fred pulled open a drawer and dug out a new logbook for Matt, "you now have 1.1 hours as a student pilot," he said as he returned to the counter after successfully hunting down the only pen in the office.

"How many hours do I need before my first solo?" Matt asked kind of nervously.

Looking up from the logbook Fred answered, "That varies from student to student. Some solo in 10 hours, others solo in 20 hours, some as many as 30. When you're ready to solo, I'll know and hopefully you'll know it too."

"I'll do take-offs and landings on my first solo, right Fred?"

Fred smiled and replied, "Yes, an equal number of each is recommended." Fred tried not to laugh at his own joke, "but seriously...yes, you will spend about 5 hours doing nothing but solo take-offs and landings before you venture out."

"Into that great unknown," Matt added.

"You'll have a map with you," Fred reassured him.

"Now don't drive down the centerline of the highway, it is not a taxiway," Fred joked with Matt as he walked to his car. "And by all means don't steer with your feet on the way home!"

Matt climbed into the driver's seat and buckled up. He gave a wave to Fred and then sped off. On his way home he drove by a few of the buildings that he had seen from the air. The school, Kay's Mart. Matt even stopped at Waffle-Burger to pick up a Belgian milkshake to help himself think. He liked those shakes; except for when the strawberries get stuck in the straw.

When Matt got home he was in a great mood! He opened up his new flight manual and reviewed all the things that they had done that day.

Later, Matt pulled the shade and tried to take a nap. He couldn't sleep though; he was too wound up from all the excitement of the day.

Chapter 2
Engine Failure?

The next day Matt had a lesson.

After their pre-flight inspection they taxied out to runway 18 and did their run-up. "Okay Matt, all of our takeoff checks are done, we've made our departure radio call and we're now looking for traffic." As Fred spoke he looked for any other airplanes in the pattern. "We can now taxi onto the runway as we check our winds again."

Fred looked over at the windsock. "We have a slight crosswind today," he began, "which means that the wind is at an angle to the runway. That can cause take-offs and landings to become more involved. We have light winds today so it won't bother us too much."

They taxied onto the runway and lined up with the centerline. Fred stopped the airplane and said, "this is a good place to stop for a moment and double check a few things before we push in the throttle."

Fred pointed at the heading indicator, "Runways are numbered according to the direction in which they run. Right now we are headed south or 180 degrees and we are on runway 18... get it?"

Matt looked surprised, "Wow, I didn't know that."

"We can recheck the heading indicator when we are aligned with the runway centerline." Fred said as he adjusted the setting knob on the instrument, "It should read 180 degrees."

Next Fred told Matt to get prepared on the rudder and push in the throttle smoothly. The engine roared as they accelerated down the runway.

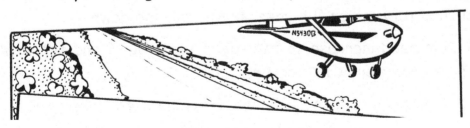

As Matt was trying to keep the airplane on the centerline, Fred pointed at the airspeed indicator and instructed him to pull back on the yoke.

First, the nose wheel rose off the pavement, then the main wheels left the runway. Matt could see the ground dropping away. He had just done his first take-off.

"You're not done yet," Fred smiled as he looked over at Matt, "we need to maintain around 75 mph. That'll give us the most altitude in the shortest amount of time in this airplane."

Matt looked at the airspeed indicator; it read 85. He pointed the nose a little higher. The airspeed dropped to 78.

"And," Fred said de-railing Matt's train of thought, "I've been holding in a little right rudder since we left the ground. At this high rpm and low airspeed, the engine torque and several other forces want to move the nose to the left. We need to hold it straight with right rudder."

"Level out at 2500 feet," Fred told Matt, "and on a heading of 270 degrees." He gave Matt a quick lesson on switching from climb to cruise.

Matt pushed forward on the yoke; the nose came down.

"Let the airspeed increase to the speed that you intend for your cruise speed before pulling back on the throttle."

When the airspeed reached 100 mph, Matt reduced the power.

"Very good, but we're heading southwest, we want to head west." Fred noted.

Matt looked down at the heading indicator. It read 240 degrees. Turning the yoke and using rudder in the same direction brought the plane to the westerly heading that Fred had requested.

Fred leaned forward and pulled out the throttle knob. "Engine failure!" he declared. The engine's rpm dropped down to an idle.

Matt's look of surprise could have easily been mistaken for terror, so Fred explained that this was only a drill. "A good pilot has to know how to handle any situation, especially an emergency situation!"

Fred straightened up in his seat and took over the controls, "I'll take this one."

Glancing at the airspeed indicator, Fred saw that the plane was going 100 mph, "70 mph is the most efficient glide speed for this airplane, so we have to slow it down." He pulled back on the yoke to raise the nose. "now for a field to land in..." Fred looked around then pointed at a field. "Also try to land into the wind but don't get into any wild maneuvers in order for that to happen. It's better to land downwind than to take a gamble. And of course we like to avoid power lines."

The ground was coming up a little faster than Matt would have liked. He hoped that they wouldn't really be landing in that field. There was a tractor in it for heaven's sake. What would the farmer think?

While Matt reconsidered the merits of taking flying lessons. Fred quickly went through the procedure for restarting a stalled engine.

"Check that both magnetos are selected and the engine primer is pushed in and locked." Fred's hand went to the items as he called them out. "The fuel tank selector should be set so as the draw out of both wing tanks. The carburetor heat knob should be pulled out and the fuel-air mixture needs to be set to the "full rich" position." Fred straightened the airplane out of it's descending spiral and started setting up for landing. "Those things I just checked could have been directly related to the engine quitting. If I had found and corrected a problem, the engine would have restarted and we could have gotten out of here."

Matt was wishing that they could get out of here. It felt really strange being so close to the ground without and airport in front of them!

"We need to make a mayday call on 121.5." Fred said as he pretended to use the radio. "Then we shut off the fuel and electrical – except the master switch. We don't shut it off until we have the flap setting that we'll need. Then we secure loose items behind us, check seat belts and then pop open the door latches. Now let's go around," he said as he pushed in the throttle.

Matt could tell Fred was hurrying through that last part.

"I usually don't get that low." Fred admitted as he looked out the window and gave a little wave to the farmer on the tractor.

"That would have been a safe landing," Fred began, "Well as safe as possible considering that was a plowed field and not a runway." Fred gave Matt back the controls while they climbed up to altitude again. "I didn't want to scare you with that simulated forced landing, but it is necessary training for every pilot."

"Have you ever had an engine failure Fred?" Matt asked.

"No I haven't." Fred replied, "Forced landings are rare. But, if I ever have a forced landing, I'll be trained for it," Fred thought for a moment, "The most important thing to remember is to stay calm and fly the airplane like it's supposed to be flown. If you fly smart, you should get through that kind of emergency just fine."

"...and I thought this plane was going to land! Sure as I'm sitting here it was headed right for my field!" Mr. Brown exclaimed to his friends."

"Did you here about that airplane that flew through George Brown's barn? It chased his cattle and almost ran down George himself!"

(How stories become exaggerated)

Chapter 3
More Lessons

Fred had Matt climb up to 3000 feet by using a climbing left turn. Matt held 75 mph and 15 degrees of bank throughout the climb. At the target altitude, Matt leveled the wings then let the nose fall in line with the horizon. After letting the full power of the engine pull the airplane up to cruising airspeed, Matt reduced the throttle.

Fred had Matt practice some more on shallow and medium bank turns.

"Did you feel that?" Fred asked Matt after completing a full circle to the right.

"That bump?" Matt replied.

Fred nodded, "you hit your own prop-wash. Your circle was so good that you came back to the same place and at the same altitude that you started. You flew through the stirred up air."

"Wow!" Matt added as he rolled into a medium bank left turn. "Let's see if I can do it again!"

Matt completed a few more turns to the left. It was quite a challenge to find his prop-wash again; he only did it once more; but Matt was having fun anyway.

"Take us back to the airport." Fred requested after glancing at his watch.

Matt leveled the wings of the airplane and looked around. Fortunately, he could still see Summit City. Matt banked to the left and headed for that small town.

"We should start descending to pattern altitude, do you remember how to come down?" asked Fred.

Matt did. Reducing the throttle was the first thing, adding back elevator pressure to control the airspeed was the next.

"Here, let's trim it." Fred said as he moved a little wheel on the instrument panel that took the pressure off the elevator. "We had better radio for airport conditions."

Matt returned to trying to figure out what that little wheel on the instrument panel did after he made that radio call.

"Oh, I'm sorry, that's the elevator trim." Fred volunteered after noticing Matt looking at the wheel, "we can add up or down trim to the elevator with that wheel. Trim adjusts the elevator so you don't have to keep holding pressure on it. It gives your arms a rest."

Fred then reminded Matt that the pattern altitude for Summit County was 1800 feet. Matt leveled out the plane when he reached that altitude.

They entered a downwind leg for runway 18. Fred had Matt make a call on the radio telling everyone their position. After the downwind and base leg, they turned onto their final approach.

"Are we going to use full flaps again?" Matt asked.

"Using the same amount of flaps for every landing is not a good habit to get into." Fred replied, "you should use the amount of flaps necessary for that particular landing." Fred leaned forward and added another 10 degrees of flaps. "That should about do it for this landing. If I were to use any more we would have to add power to make the runway."

Matt followed Fred along on the controls as they made another smooth landing.

"You're doing just fine Matt, you'll be soloing before you know it." Fred indicated to Matt to take over taxiing the airplane.

Matt smiled. "Think of it," he thought to himself, me, flying solo. Matt turned the wheel in front of him toward the approaching taxiway. Nothing happened.

Fred pushed in on the rudder pedal and the plane turned toward the parking area, "Don't worry Matt, you still have lots of hours to practice before then."

"Don't forget!" Fred called after Matt, "ground school starts Saturday."

Matt waved and drove off. He was on the schedule for Thursday and Friday, but it was supposed to rain for the next few days and Fred said it probably wouldn't be VFR conditions. Matt had agreed with him except that he didn't know what VFR meant. "Visual Flight Rules," Fred answered Matt, "we can't fly unless we can see three miles, and for a flight lesson, I like at least 10 miles of visibility."

Fred explained to Matt that with advanced training and more advanced instrumentation in the airplane you can fly by Instrument Flight Rules. IFR means that you can fly the airplane through a cloud, a whole bunch of clouds. It means that you can fly for hours without being able to see out the window.

Matt turned into his apartment complex, parked and went in. He needed to start getting ready for work. Matt worked second shift as a candy tester for a big confections manufacturer. It was a good job. He just wished they offered dental insurance.

That night at Matt's place of employment...

"So you're learning how to fly," Matt's friend Maynerd said to him between flavors of "Jumpin' Jo Jo Beez".

Matt nodded at Maynerd while he chewed down his "Everlastin' Caramel Caravan Surprise." "It's incredible, you should try it," he said taking a big swig of "Maple Pop." "There's nothing like flying." With that he popped a couple of "Red Hot Chew-Noble Fusion Reactors" into his mouth.

Maynerd took a moment six-tenths of the way through his "Mile-O-Licorice" to say "Maybe I'll learn how to fly too, It sounds really cool."

The "Multi-Mega-Ton Marshmallow Marble" that Matt had in his mouth blew up. It was ten times it's original size and Matt couldn't get his mouth shut. He made a note of this in his quality control book.

Maynerd was on number three of his box of "Ten Command-Mints" when he looked at his watch and said, "Good, it's almost lunch time!"

It did rain the next day. But Fred had quite a few things to do around the office anyway. He had a computer problem he needed to solve. He had been planning to build shelves along the back wall; not to mention putting a new coat of paint on the walls of the classroom. It took Fred 10 minutes to decide on what to do. He curled up on the couch and took a nap.

Friday cleared up nicely, giving Matt a chance to take another lesson. They reviewed climbs, descents, medium bank turns and steep banked turns. Then Fred started to talk about the effects of the wind.

"Try and follow that road." Fred pointed down at a straight eastbound road just off their nose.

Matt could line the airplane up with the country road but they kept drifting off to the north.

"We are heading east at 100 miles an hour. The air that we are flying through is headed north at 10," Fred explained. "If we were to continue flying like this for an hour we would be not only 100 miles east of here but 10 miles north as well."

Matt thought about what Fred had told him a few days ago about how wind effects the speed over the ground and added, "If we were to fly directly south into that wind our speed over the ground would be 10 miles an hour less."

"Correct, it would be like swimming upstream," Fred answered.

Fred reminded Matt that if you wanted to canoe straight across a river you would have to point the bow of the boat slightly upstream.

Matt related that to his problem and pointed the plane's nose slightly south of that country road and followed it with not problem.

Fred had Matt fly a rectangle course around a big field. Each side of the course presented a different wind problem.

"Now we're on the downwind leg," Fred announced as Matt leveled the wings from the previous turn, "our ground speed is high because we are going with the wind. On our next turn we will need to use a steep bank because of our high ground speed."

"We need to turn quickly or else we will cover too much ground." Matt added.

"We also need to turn quickly because there's more than 90 degrees to cover," Fred began, "It's like when you tried to follow that road, you had to point your nose slightly upwind to maintain a straight path over the ground. We will need to complete the turn plus add a little, to correct for the crosswind."

The next two turns required a shallow bank. The turn after that was steep. Matt looked a little confused so Fred told him to look over his flight manual's section on wind maneuvers when he got home; that will help a lot.

"This exercise will help train you to fly a good, safe traffic pattern; where a straight track over the ground is necessary," Fred explained.

"Next thing we're going to do," Fred began, "is to see how slowly this airplane will fly. Minimum Controllable Airspeed is flight right on the edge of a stall."

Matt recalled the stall Fred had showed him a few days ago; how the nose dropped and he had gotten that roller coaster feeling.

"Developing a feel for slow speed flight is really important for safety," Fred said as he added in a touch more power. "Our airspeeds are lowest during take offs and landings. Oddly enough that's also when we're closest to the ground where there's no room for mistakes."

Matt thought that made a lot of sense. You could lose 200 feet in a stall recovery and get away with it here at 2400 feet above the ground, but during a take off or landing you wouldn't have the altitude to recover, so you certainly don't want to stall near the ground.

"I'm going to hold our 3000 feet of altitude," Fred said as he reduced the throttle. "It will require more and more up elevator to keep that altitude." He put down full flaps when the airspeed slowed enough, relaxing elevator pressure as they came in. Fred then added plenty of engine power to hold that nose high; very slow flight.

The plane was flying at 44 mph and the nose was pointing way above the horizon. It sounded like the engine was working way to hard and Matt couldn't see a thing out of the front window. It didn't seem very efficient. Fred pointed out that their speed over the ground was probably only 20 mile an hour; since they were flying into the wind.

Fred recovered from the slow flight attitude by adding full power, pushing forward on the yoke and letting the nose fall to level. He then slowly retracted the flaps. After the airplane's speed increased to cruising speed, Fred reduced the power. "This time it's your airplane to fly." Fred looked at Matt and said, "I'll help you through it."

Matt really had to work on the rudder pedals during slow flight. He also had to constantly adjust the throttle and elevator. "This is a lot of work," he confessed to Fred.

"You're doing fine," Fred replied. "Now let's try a gentle turn to the left."

They recovered from the slow flight maneuvers that they had been practicing and headed back to the airport. After doing three "touch and go's", they did their full stop landing and taxied back to the hanger.

Matt figured that he didn't have very much to do with those landings. He figured Fred had actually landed the plane each time.

"Are you kidding?" Fred acted surprised when Matt brought it up, "I just made a few corrections. You were in control. Besides, you've seen me land. I land better than that." Fred chuckled as he thought of his own bounced landings. Most of them had been in his student days, but more than enough had been well after that. He bounced one last week and told his student that he had done it on purpose just to illustrate a point.

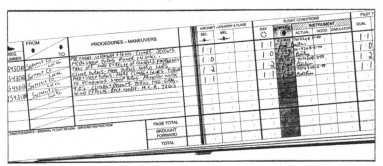

Matt liked the way the hours added up in his logbook. He looked at the schedule and signed himself up for another lesson tomorrow.

Matt thought that he would sit on the porch of the airport office for a while before heading home. He had heard the pilot of a King-Air call in earlier and ask for an airport advisory. Matt thought that he would hang around and watch the big twin engine airplane land.

While Matt was waiting, he saw a little dog run out from under a pine tree nearby the hanger, sit down in the grass and turn it's attention toward the northeast.

A moment later the King-Air pilot's voice boomed over the airport's outside speaker. He said that he was 5 miles to the northeast and would be landing on runway 18.

Sure enough; Matt spotted the airplane in the same section of sky that the dog had been watching. Matt noticed the dog's head followed the motion of the King-Air as it used up most of the runway during its landing roll. The big plane taxied off of the runway and parked on the ramp. When the pilot shut down the airplane's two engines, the airport was quiet.

The dog chased a butterfly for a moment or two then wandered back under that pine tree.

The next day as Matt pre-flighted the airplane he looked over at that pine tree to see if the dog was there; it wasn't. Matt went back to checking out the airplane.

Fred joined Matt a little later. They started the plane and taxied out to the runway.

"There's good 'ol Spinner." Fred said as he pointed out his window at the dog sitting beside the pine tree. "He's afraid of people, but loves airplanes."

Matt smiled. The little dog looked kind of cute sitting over there watching them.

"We give him food and water," Fred began, "he doesn't bother us or anything. He won't even let us pet him. Spinner just likes to watch airplanes."

Matt taxied onto the runway and pushed in the throttle knob.

Spinner watched as the Cessna flew off into the distance.

After practicing slow flight again and a couple of steep turns, Fred had Matt go right into some power-off stalls.

The stall warning buzzer started to go off and Fred instructed Matt to pull back further on the yoke. Matt held his breath and pulled back that last little bit.

That did it. The plane stopped flying. The nose of the airplane dropped down and pointed at the ground 2500 feet below and Matt got that roller coaster feeling again.

Matt released the back pressure on the yoke that he had been holding in and, with Fred's prompting, pushed in on the throttle knob to bring back full power from the engine. The plane gained airspeed and he pulled the nose up.

"Not bad," Fred said as he pointed at the altimeter. "But we lost 200 feet of altitude. We need to cut that down to about 50 feet."

They continued to practice stalls for a while. After that Fred asked Matt to take him back to the airport and show him some more landings. They would be discussing stalls at ground school tonight anyway.

During the last landing, Matt remembered to look over by the hanger. Spinner was out watching. He was sitting by his tree.

That night at ground school Fred began to introduce everyone.

"Marcie, Mr. Willard, Doc Goldsmith," Fred paused when he got to Matt's friend.

"This is my friend Maynerd, he works with me," Matt told Fred.

"Maynerd, Matt, Mrs. Whirley,"

"Please call me Shirley," Mrs Whirly asked Fred.

"Surely," Fred continued. "welcome the Summit County Aviation Ground School."

"Will we get a break?" Maynerd asked after raising his hand.

Fred shook his head, "Yes, we will take a break. This will be a relaxing classroom; we'll learn but we will try to make it fun too."

Fred explained about the FAA written test that they must pass before they could get their pilot's license. He explained that the test would cover aerodynamics, weather, navigation, rules and regulations, instruments, engines, aircraft performance and other related subjects. Fred said that it would take a lot of studying, but reminded everyone that aviation is a very interesting subject to study. Matt agreed and opened his book to chapter one.

"There's going to be a lot of stuff to learn." Matt said to Maynerd as they headed home from the airport.

"The written test should be easy," Maynerd began, "Fred said that the FAA will only ask us 50 questions."

"Out of over 700 possible questions!" Matt stated, "we are going to have to know everything about everything."

Maynerd's expression turned a bit sour. "You mean that they won't tell us which 50 questions to study for?"

"No Maynerd, they won't." Matt answered quietly.

"Well I scored 50 on my driving test," Maynerd said proudly, "I can do it on this test too."

Matt kept quiet and didn't remind Maynerd that it was 50% he had scored on his driving test and not 50 out of 50. "We will study together," Matt said turning to his friend. "I know that both of us can do it if we try hard enough."

Maynerd nodded in agreement as he pushed in a tape that played the theme music from Top Gun.

A very strong east wind blew all day Sunday. Fred told Matt that it was too early in his training to fly in such a strong crosswind. Fred said that Matt should learn how to land under normal conditions before he tackled something a little more tricky; like a wind that wants to blow you off the side of the runway.

Matt stayed home and studied the chapter on aerodynamics in his ground school study book. Then he read ahead into the chapter about airplane performance. After lunch he opened the flight training manual and read about all the maneuvers that they had practiced the week previous. Matt was amazed at how much they had covered.

In their last few flights they had practiced power-on stalls, power-off stalls and flying on the edge of a stall during slow flight. Matt shook his head in quiet embarrassment when he recalled his first lesson when he had tried to gain 500 feet by using the elevator alone. Fred had made him continue his quest for altitude until the airspeed dropped so low that the plane just stopped flying and the nose fell, pointing at the earth below. Matt had learned that when he wanted to gain altitude he had better use the throttle.

Matt folded a paper airplane out of a Publishers Clearing House envelope and tossed it across the room. Ironically it landed in the trash can. "Sorry about that," Matt said as he hurried over and lifted the plane out. He could see Ed's face smiling up at him. Matt hoped that this wouldn't effect his chances for the big prize.

After making a runway on the floor out of stamps with the names of magazines on them Matt practiced his airport traffic patterns. He then took Ed's private jet up to altitude and practiced his turns, climbs and glides.

All through the next week Fred had Matt practice everything they had learned so far. Matt still didn't feel comfortable about a lot of things. Take-offs and landings were probably the hardest thing for him to get used to. Fred told Matt he was doing fine.

"You have the runway made," Fred stated, "pull out the power and add more flaps."

Matt moved the flap lever all the way down. As the flaps came in he had to apply a little forward pressure against the yoke to keep the nose from coming up to much.

"Don't forget to flare," Fred reminded Matt about 20 feet above the runway.

Matt eased back on the yoke which resulted in the nose of the airplane raising up through level.

"Keep it off," Fred whispered, "The main wheels should touch down gently."

And the main wheels did touch gently.

"That was nice," Matt complimented himself. It did feel really good to finally flare properly. Matt had been trying to do it that smoothly for what seemed like weeks.

"I know I told you that we would make that our last landing for the day," Fred began, "but that last one was so good we need to see if you can do it again."

Matt raised the flap handle, turned off the carburetor heat and pushed in the throttle making that airplane race forward; taking to the sky once more.

"SUMMIT COUNTY CESSNA 3 DELTA BRAVO ON DOWNWIND FOR RUNWAY 18."

Matt delivered that radio call with confidence then rechecked his altitude and alignment with the runway.

Fred leaned over and pulled out the throttle, leaving the engine to idle uselessly. "Engine out," Fred said politely.

"SUMMIT COUNTY CESSNA 3 DELTA BRAVO, SIMULATED ENGINE FAILURE ON DOWNWIND, RUNWAY 18"

Fred made the radio call while Matt continued the descending turn. He brought the plane over the runway and lined up with the centerline. Pulling back on the yoke Matt flared the plane. The touch-down was a little hard and they bounced back up into the air again. After settling in for one last bounce they finally stayed on the runway.

Fred gave Matt another chance to practice a normal landing. He promised not to do anything to interrupt him this time. Matt's landing this time was quite nice.

After parking the airplane and discussing the day's lesson with Fred, Matt relaxed on the porch. Ground school was going to start in an hour or so anyway. He would just hang around the airport.

Spinner was out, Matt noticed a few minutes later, chasing butterflies again; he kinda spun around in circles trying to catch them. Matt decided to go over and see if they could become friends.

He went out onto the grass beside the hanger. The little dog stopped what he was doing and watched Matt's every move.

"Hello Spinner," Matt said and then sat down in the grass.

Matt talked to him gently. The puppy dog's ears were perked up the whole time that he talked. He seemed interested but wouldn't come any closer though.

Matt laid back on the soft grass and shut his eyes. The feeling of the warm sun and gentle wind on him was pretty relaxing.

Ten minutes later Kristen looked out of the airport's office window and noticed Matt sound asleep on the grass with his hat pulled down over his eyes. Spinner was chasing butterflies not more than 5 feet away.

The next thing Matt knew, Maynerd was standing over him saying something about class starting in a few minutes.

"This is a wing flying along at a high angle of attack," Fred pointed at the picture on the left, "and this is a wing flying along at a low angle of attack."

Matt resumed taking notes alongside the duck with cowboy boots he had drawn during Fred's explanation to Maynerd's question on how they get the lead inside a pencil.

Chapter 4

Going Solo?

Chapter 4

Going Solo?

As the next week's lessons progressed, Matt was starting to get nervous. Fred had told Matt not to wear too nice of a shirt for the next few lessons. Matt was pretty sure he knew why; he had noticed all the cut-out T-shirt backs on the wall of the airport office. They had the name and the date of a pilot's first solo written on them.

"Why don't you just pull off the runway at the next taxiway and let me out?" Fred asked Matt after only about a half hour of touch-and-go's later that week.

Well, Matt could think of a dozen reasons why Fred should not get out of the airplane, but he didn't bring them up. Matt found some courage, pulled off onto a taxiway and braked to a stop.

"Do three take-offs and landings to a full stop," Fred explained, "that means pulling off after each landing and taxiing back to the start of the runway." Fred didn't look up from signing Matt's logbook until he smiled and said, "then you can taxi back to the hanger and shut it down."

Fred popped open the door and stepped out. Matt checked that the door was secure like Fred had told him.

Fred watched for a moment as the plane started to taxi. He then turned and headed back to the office.

Matt stopped the airplane just short of the runway. He went over his before-take-off-checklist and made his radio call, after he looked for other traffic.

"SUMMIT COUNTY TRAFFIC, CESSNA FIVE FOUR THREE DELTA BRAVO, DEPARTING RUNWAY 18"

Matt added a little power and the plane taxied onto the runway, rolled onto the giant numbers that were painted on the pavement and smoothly lined up with the centerline.

Matt stared down that centerline with excitement. He knew that he was just a push on the throttle knob away from flying an airplane all on his own. It was so exhilarating. Matt was starting to feel more confident as he reached down for that throttle. He knew what to do. He had done what seemed like hundreds of take-offs and landings in the last few days.

Matt thought a moment about how proud he would be telling people about what he was about to do.

He slid his feet off the brakes, smiled assuredly then pushed in the throttle.

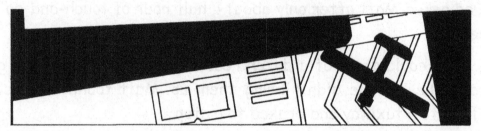

The airplane thundered down the runway. Matt glanced down at the airspeed indicator and saw it climb through 55 mph. He pulled back on the yoke to raise the nose wheel off the pavement. Seconds later the whole plane lifted off into the air. After establishing the best rate of climb Matt looked behind him to make sure he was still lined up with the runway and not drifting to the left or right. He was right where he should be, he had corrected for the wind properly.

The world was falling below and at the same time opening up in front of him. "The horizon is always at eye level," Fred had told Matt, "but the higher you go the more stuff it contains."

The air was clear. He could see for miles and miles. Matt could see the shadows of a half a dozen puffy clouds move silently across the otherwise sunny landscape. He could see a lake glistening in the distance and a fisherman fishing in a pond right below him, To his right,...

It suddenly sank in that there was no-one sitting to his right. That seat was empty. Matt was flying this thing all by himself. It was up to him to bring it back for a landing. Matt straightened up in his seat. Looked for traffic then turned onto the crosswind leg of the traffic pattern. Matt leveled out when he reached 1800 feet.

He wasn't sure if it was a feeling of pride, the fear of death or the onion dip he had eaten for breakfast that made Matt's stomach feel like it did; but whatever it was seemed to get worse the more he thought about being alone at the controls of this airplane. A month ago he didn't even know what a traffic pattern was and now he was turning downwind for runway 18. "Go figure", he thought, "I hope I'm ready." Matt realized that this was a heck of a time to question his abilities. "Fred must think that I'm ready," he reassured himself. "Fred wouldn't let me solo if I wasn't." And with that Matt looked out at the familiar picture of the runway off to his left just like he had seen so many times before and made his downwind call.

"SUMMIT COUNTY TRAFFIC THREE DELTA BRAVO DOWNWIND FOR RUNWAY 18."

A woman's voice radiated from the radio.

"SUMMIT COUNTY TRAFFIC CHEROKEE SEVEN TWO NINER SIERRA ALPHA ON EXTENDED LEFT BASE FOR 18."

Matt looked out to his right and could faintly see an airplane approaching from the east. Fred and Matt had encountered other traffic in the pattern before but usually Fred would help Matt through it. This time Matt was on his own.

He pulled out the carb heat and reduced the power. As Matt slowed down to descent speed he took another look at the airplane in the distance.

"SUMMIT COUNTY TRAFFIC CESSNA THREE DELTA BRAVO TURNING BASE FOR RUNWAY 18, TRAFFIC IN SIGHT."

Matt rolled the wings level and reduced the power.

"SUMMIT COUNTY TRAFFIC CHEROKEE NINER SIERRA ALPHA ALSO HAS TRAFFIC IN SIGHT. WILL FOLLOW THE CESSNA IN FOR LANDING."

Matt smiled and thought to himself that his was too cool. "It really feels like I'm a pilot now."

After checking for other traffic, Matt turned onto the final approach. He reduced power and added more flaps, then checked his seat belt just to be sure.

Matt pulled the throttle to idle when he knew that he had the runway made. Smoothly applying the up elevator brought the plane through level and for a moment Matt held it just inches above the runway.

"I'm going to do it," Matt thought to himself, "I'm going to live through my first solo flight."

Fred watched Matt's first solo landing from the office window. With binoculars Fred could see Matt's expression change from one of serious concentration during the flare, to a really excited smile after the plane had landed. Fred put down the binoculars and folded his arms across his chest. Fred looked pleased.

After Matt completed his three take-off's and landings, he taxied the airplane off of the runway and headed for the hanger. Matt parked the plane and shut it down.

"Good job Matt," Fred shouted as he walked toward him from the office. Matt could see that Fred had a pair of scissors in his hand. "Why don't you turn around and put both hands on the engine cowling for me?"

Matt did what Fred had suggested. Moments later Matt could feel a breeze behind him that wasn't there before.

Fred smiled as he shook Matt's hand, "Congratulations, you should be very proud."

Matt couldn't get the smile off of his face all the way home. On the way he stopped at his friend Maynerd's place to show off his newly modified shirt.

Maynerd suggested that they call a few friends and go out on the town to celebrate.

"Another round for the pilot here," Matt's friend Terry said to the bartender.

"I think he's had enough," the barkeep replied and went back to wiping his counter.

Matt stared straight ahead with utter amazement of how strong an ice cream headache can get. There were twelve empty banana split boats scattered around the large table and six of them had been Matt's.

"Well at least he's gotten his daily allowance of potassium," Woody commented thinking of all those bananas.

Maynerd drove Matt home to change his shirt and get ready for work. Matt didn't really feel like going to work today, seeing that all that sweet stuff had given him quite a belly ache. Matt went to work anyway, although he was wishing that he had picked some other profession than a candy taster.

Chapter 5
The Cross Countries

All Matt did for the next two lessons was solo take offs and landings. He certainly didn't mind, those were a lot of fun, but Matt had a terrible urge to break away from the airport and really go out and do some flying.

"How would you like to do more than just touch-and-go's today?" Fred said to Matt when he arrived for his next lesson.

Matt smiled and replied, "You bet I would!"

Fred told Matt to do a couple of take-offs and landings then climb out to 2500 feet. "Since we went over aeronautical charts in ground school, you should have no problem finding Bakersfield, Allmont and Gunn Lake." Fred pointed out the towns on the chart that he wanted Matt to find.

"Just fly over them, but don't land there?" Matt asked as he picked up the airplane keys.

"Right, just fly over them," Fred answered, "the main purpose of this flight is for you to get familiar with your chart and the way landmarks are depicted on it." Fred paused, "and of course to return safely."

"Of course," Matt agreed as he walked out the door.

Matt had a good time. He flew over Summit on his way to Bakersfield. When he arrived above Bakersfield Matt did a steep turn over the downtown area. How many hundreds of people would be looking up at him? Matt wondered as he looked down onto the busy square. Matt leveled the wings and then headed south to Allmont.

It was really a terrific feeling to be in complete control of that airplane. Matt felt so proud as he flew over all of those towns, lakes and farms. Matt could see the sky line of Anytown U.S.A. (which by the way is where John Doe and his wife Jane lives.) "I really should go visit good ol' John and his wife one of these days," Matt thought to himself.

He didn't worry about getting lost. Matt never lost sight of Summit since it was such a clear day. It made him feel good to still be able to see his home town in the distance, but Matt knew that he would have to leave the security of this practice area when he did his solo cross-countries. It sure must be easy to get lost up here Matt thought as he tried to figure out which town in the distance was Gunn lake.

Matt picked the one with a lake next to it shaped like a gun.

"SUMMIT COUNTY UNICOM, CESSNA 543 DELTA BRAVO, FIVE MILES SOUTH-EAST, REQUESTING AIRPORT ADVISORY."

Matt could see the airport in the distance as he made his radio call. A moment later Kristen, the Office Manager's voice radiated from the speaker. She gave Matt the wind direction and speed, active runway and reported that there wasn't any other traffic in the area.

"Thank goodness," Matt thought to himself as he reduced the power to descend to pattern altitude. Matt was wishing that he hadn't drank quite so many cans of soda-pop before he arrived at the airport this afternoon.

Fred saw the determination in Matt's eyes when he walked, rather quickly, into the office. Fred understood that look; he had been there himself many times. Fred waited until Matt emerged from the restroom before he asked him about the flight.

Matt and Fred talked for an hour about the flight. Fred had Matt point out some of the things on the aeronautical chart that helped him navigate. Fred also showed him some other things on the chart that would help him in the future. Matt successfully folded up his chart on only the third attempt and then asked Fred what was next.

"You and I have to go on a trip," Fred replied to Matt's question, "time to start your cross-countries."

Both Fred and Matt would fly together on the first cross-country flight. Matt would then do three more trips by himself. The last one would be Matt's long cross-country, with each landing point at least 100 miles away from the starting airport.

"They will all need to be tower controlled airports," Fred added, "we will be flying with the big airplanes."

It is not required to land at all tower controlled airports on your cross-countries, but Fred told Matt that the best way to overcome the fear of larger airports is to jump right in and learn how those larger airports operate.

Matt could hardly wait. He just hoped that their little Cessna wouldn't get sucked into the intake of a Jumbo-Jet.

The morning sun was just rising as Matt drove to the airport the next day. He had stayed up late the night before figuring out headings and distances for the cross-country flight that they were making today. Matt wasn't awake yet. He would have stopped for coffee except he figured that coffee, cool air and a long, possible bumpy flight wouldn't go together too well. Matt stuck his head out of the window instead.

Fred had Matt call weather when he arrived. With that information Matt could figure out what heading to fly, how long each leg of the trip would take and how much fuel would be necessary. Matt filled all that information in on his planning sheet and gave it to Fred to check over.

Using Matt's plotter and flight computer, Fred checked all of Matt's headings, times and distances. "Good job Matt," Fred praised his student, "I think we're ready for our trip."

Matt gathered all the stuff he needed in a organized clump. Fred grabbed the keys to the airplane and they both headed out the door.

After taking off, Fred had Matt do a climbing left turn until they reached 2500 feet. Matt started his stopwatch as they passed over the airport and were heading towards their first destination.

"This leg of the trip is pretty easy," Matt commented, "all I have to do is follow the highway north until it passes the airport."

Fred glanced at Matt's chart then replied, "it will still be a good idea to keep an eye on your checkpoints, taking a note of your times between them," Fred explained, "that will tell us our speed over the ground and if the forecasted winds at this altitude are accurate," Fred paused for a moment, "and besides, it will be good practice for the next leg which won't be so easy."

Matt agreed. There wasn't much else but woods and a couple lakes between the next two airports. He would worry about that later, Right now Matt had to prepare to talk to a control tower. Matt had practiced his airline captain's voice for a few hours last night. He had also practiced it in his car on the way to the airport this morning. People had given Matt strange looks when they saw him talking to his thumb.

"We are 20 miles away from St. Helen's," Fred announced, "You had better contact the control tower."

Matt tuned in the Terminal Information Frequency before contacting Approach Control. A recorded message gave them the current weather, runway in use and a lot of other information that would help them on their flight in. Fred told Matt that it was a really good idea to write all this information down. Matt dug out one of the five pencils that he had brought along with him and started to write. The recording ended with, "you have information Foxtrot."

"You should tell approach that you have information Foxtrot," Fred explained, "they update the information often and call it a different name each time; so basically you are letting them know that you have the current information."

Fred coached Matt on what to say to approach.

"ST. HELEN APPROACH, CESSNA 543 DELTA BRAVO, 18 MILES SOUTH, INBOUND FOR LANDING WITH INFORMATION POLKA."

"Foxtrot," Fred corrected.

"FOXTROT."

The controller instructed Matt to continue on his present course and announce when he makes visual contact with the airport.

"CESSNA 3 DELTA BRAVO HAS AIRPORT IN SIGHT."

Matt did what the controller said and switched over to the tower frequency.

"ST HELEN TOWER, CESSNA 3 DELTA BRAVO IS WITH YOU."

Matt rolled in some aileron and stepped on the rudder pedal banking the airplane and dropping that left wing right in front of Fred's view of the runway.

Fred had been watching a business jet taxi out onto the runway, preparing to take-off. When Matt leveled the wings after reaching the heading for their base leg, Fred's view was clear again. He could see the runway. The sleek jet was already off the ground and rocketing its way into the sky. It was amazing how much power that jet had; a few moments later it disappeared into a cloud.

The controller in the tower cleared them to land. Matt glanced quickly for other traffic then turned onto the final approach. Matt lined up the airplane onto the centerline of that huge runway and made an almost perfect landing.

Matt returned home in time to attend the family get-together that his mom had planned for that night. It was hard for Matt not to brag too much about his flying lessons, since he was still pretty wound up from all the excitement of the day. Everyone was either polite or very interested in hearing about Matt's flying.

Uncle Milton stated that he might start taking flying lessons. Aunt Josie said that she thought it would be wonderful to soar with the birds. Matt's mom even said that she was planning on going for a ride with Matt when he gets his license. Matt's little brother Ben wondered how long it would take Matt to notice that he had his tie dipped in his soup.

After dinner Matt pulled out his airplane stuff and started to plan his solo cross country. "Gee, I hope nobody noticed," Matt said to himself after his spotted the tomato soup stain on his white tie.

The first thing Matt did was to unfold his chart and get an overview of his trip coming up tomorrow. It sure covered a lot of distance. Matt did a quick calculation and discovered the trip would cover over two hundred miles. Two hundred miles of flying by himself, over unfamiliar terrain and landing at unfamiliar airports. Actually Matt was getting quite excited about it. He knew that he hadn't ever done anything so thrilling in his life. Except, Matt thought, maybe the time a few summers ago when his friend Calvin talked him into riding a wagon down the mogul run on Whish-Ski Mountain. Matt winced when he recalled the unique feeling that hundreds of pine needles in your shorts can give you.

"Anyway," Matt uttered as he leaned over his aeronautical chart again, trying to refocus his attention on his upcoming flight. A moment later Matt took out his pencil and plotter and began drawing true course lines on the chart.

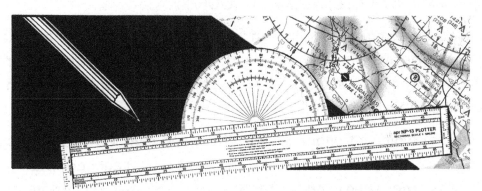

"It's a beautiful day for a cross-country flight," Fred announced as Matt walked into the airport office.

Matt pulled out his planning sheet and showed it to Fred. After looking it over Fred handed it back to Matt and said, "all we need to do now is to call Flight Service and get the weather."

For the second day in a row Matt dialed the number for Flight Service.

This time Matt identified himself as a student pilot and the weather person on the phone now knew how to talk to Matt; slowly and clearly. Matt had time to write down all the weather information that was given to him and was able to understand all of that information. Matt thanked the operator for being so helpful and then hung up the phone.

Knowing what the winds were going to be at the altitude Matt planned to fly, he could calculate his time between airports and also what headings to fly to get to those airports.

Fred figured that Matt must have spent a lot of time practicing with his flight computer because all of Matt's heading and time enroutes were figured correctly. Fred signed Matt's logbook stating that Matt was ready for this solo cross-country. He handed the logbook back to Matt and wished him a good flight. Fred sat down in one of the office chairs and watched Matt walk proudly out to the airplane with a load of paperwork under his arm.

"SUMMIT COUNTY TRAFFIC, CESSNA 543 DELTA BRAVO, DEPARTING RUNWAY 36, SUMMIT COUNTY."

Matt checked again for other traffic in the area and then proceeded to taxi onto the active runway. He lined up with the centerline and then pushed in the throttle smoothly. A matter of moments later the small airplane was climbing into the sky.

Matt kept the airport under him as the plane climbed in a wide spiral up to the altitude that he planned to fly. When he reached that altitude, Matt leveled the wings and started off in the direction that his calculations told him would get him to his first destination. Looking down Matt started his stopwatch as he passed over Summit Airport.

"Take your time over the airport," Matt remembered Fred saying at the same point in yesterday's flight. Matt had given Fred a strange look; he couldn't understand why Fred had wanted him to fly slowly over the airport.

Fred figured out why Matt looked confused, smiled and pointed at his watch, "take note of your time when we pass over the airport."

Matt remembered being a little embarrassed about the mistake but Fred didn't rub it in too much. Today Matt was on his own, he would have to laugh at his own mistakes; although Matt wasn't planning on making any.

I'm on the correct heading, I've been holding my altitude steady at 2500 feet and I see my first big checkpoint off in the distance. Matt smiled as he took note of his early successes.

Matt's smile quickly faded when he thought about all that was ahead of him. It made Matt a little nervous to know that he was going to have to talk to at least a half a dozen controllers on this trip, not to mention that he would be flying in the same area with all those commercial airliners. Matt straightened up in his seat, glanced over at the passengers seat which was now serving as his office desk. He double checked that all the things that he would need were easy to access.

When Matt arrived over Millersburg, his first checkpoint, Matt wrote down the time that had elapsed since he took his time over Summit Airport. Matt then pulled out his flight computer and lined up the distance on the outer dial with the time on the inner dial. It had taken Matt 11 minutes to fly 23 miles. There is a good tailwind, Matt thought to himself, my speed over the ground is 125 mph.

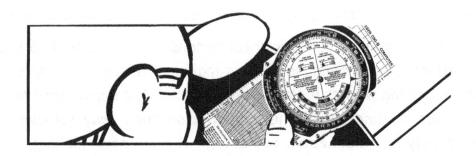

"Oh my goodness!" Matt exclaimed almost dropping his chart onto the cockpit floor, "I have to call up Approach Control."

He had been so busy making sure that he wasn't lost by looking for every radio antenna, railroad track or gravel pit that the chart said he would fly over; that Matt almost forgot about using the radio.

"GRAND RAPIDS APPROACH, CESSNA 543 DELTA BRAVO..."

Matt could've kicked himself. He had just broadcast over the wrong frequency. If Summit airport wasn't out of range. Fred should be getting a good laugh right now.

Moving the radio dial to the correct frequency this time, Matt let Grand Rapids Approach know that he was inbound for landing. The controller at Grand Rapids told Matt to continue on his present course until he spotted the airport.

After a couple of minutes the controller's voice came over the radio again, "CESSNA 3 DELTA BRAVO, DO YOU HAVE THE AIRPORT?"

Matt said that he could not see the airport yet. The controller told Matt to look at his 11:00.

When Matt looked just to the left of the nose he saw the airport and proudly told the controller that he had the airport in sight.

"CESSNA 3 DELTA BRAVO CLEAR TO LAND."

Matt studied the massive airport in front of him. Two miles of runway, in which Matt would only use a thousand feet. As Matt slowly descended down to that huge expanse of pavement he saw one of the reasons why this airport needed such a long runway; there was a 737 waiting for him to land.

Matt wasn't sure if he felt powerful because he could hold up such a big plane or self-conscious because he was making these busy people wait for him. Matt; a person who still slept in pajamas with a super hero printed on the front, was holding up all these people on their way somewhere. The pilot, who surely had a schedule to keep must have been looking out of the window patiently waiting waiting for Matt to get this slow flying plane onto the ground and off of the runway.

As he should have, Matt concentrated on landing his plane safely and not looking to see if the pilot or any of the passengers of that airliner were watching his landing. If they had been, Matt made it a good one.

Captain N. Teneel had watched Matt's landing and thought it had looked pretty smooth. He was looking forward to flying his own light airplane this weekend.

Most of the passengers hadn't noticed the small plane land. Especially Brutus, who sat in the first window seat. Brutus was trying to open a small bag of peanuts that the stewardess had brought him. Brutus was hungry.

Behind Brutus sat Tom. Tom was trying to picture his far away, calm place as his psychologist had suggested. Tom was afraid to fly.

Behind Tom sat Deb. Deb loved to throw water-balloons from the balcony of her 12th story apartment. Deb brought a water-balloon just in case she could get the window open. Deb was a nut.

Behind Deb two boys were fighting over a window seat.

Behind the two boys sat Ed of Big Ed's muffler shop. Ed was napping. Big Ed had a busy day selling mufflers at a convention. Big Ed was exhausted.

Matt switched to the radio frequency for Ground Control after the tower instructed him to do so. They cleared Matt to taxi to Zippy's Aviation which was the place that Fred had told Matt to stop in and have someone sign his logbook.

As Matt taxied parallel to the runway he couldn't help but notice that the airliner that had been waiting for him was now taking off. He heard the roar of those massive engines switch from loud to thunderous and ground shaking as the big airplane passed Matt up pointing the business ends of those jet exhausts so Matt could see the fire inside. Matt watched the 737 accelerate down the runway and slowly lift its nose into the air. Seconds later the airliner was rocketing it's way into the sky at what seemed like an impossible angle.

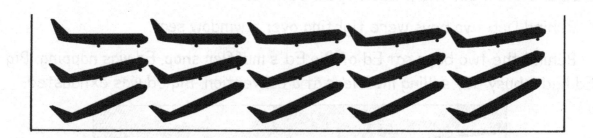

Matt turned right on the next taxiway as instructed by Ground Control and headed for Zippy's Aviation.

"Welcome to Zippy's," the woman behind the counter said to Matt as he walked through the door.

It was a really nice place. Matt stood in a plush lobby with several rooms off of it. There was a pilot's lounge being used by several pilots lounging. A lunch room with vending machines and tables to eat at. There were restrooms of course and another room marked "Flight Planning" - through the window of that room Matt noticed a computer monitor, a phone, some books laying around and a big map on the wall.

Matt asked to have his logbook signed by Kay; the woman behind the desk. As she was signing the book, Matt looked at all the neat stuff in the display case.

"Will there be anything else?" she asked.

Matt bought a hat that looked like one an airline captain would wear. He took off his old hat and proudly switched it with his new one. He thanked Kay and walked out the door. Matt hoped his new hat would bring him luck.

As Matt walked across the pavement towards the airplane, he tried to comprehend the moment; here he was over a hundred miles from home, at a busy airport in a town that Matt had never been to before. "And I flew here! Imagine that," Matt thought to himself, "a few months ago I hardly knew anything about airplanes and now this airplane that I am walking towards is my ride home. I sure have come a long way."

Thinking about the magnificence of the situation reminded Matt that his nerves were still on alert status as they had been throughout this whole trip. Matt took a deep breath and walked on.

Even though Matt had only been out of the plane for a few minutes, he was taught to still perform a walk around check of the airplane before entering. Besides, the habit might someday save him the embarrassment of trying to taxi without removing the wheel chocks or something silly like that. Matt was all for safety and avoiding embarrassment.

Before starting the engine, Matt set up the passenger seat like a desk again and prepared to call up the controller that would give him clearance to fly onto his next destination.

"GRAND RAPID'S CLEARANCE, THIS IS CESSNA 543 DELTA BRAVO."

"CESSNA 543 DELTA BRAVO CLEARED TO MIDVILLE, VFR 2500 FEET, SQUAWK 2337, DEPARTURE FREQUENCY 128.05." Matt read back in condensed form the clearance that had been given to him over the radio by Clearance Delivery.

As he reached forward to set the number in the transponder that he was told to "squawk" Matt smiled a bit; he had thought that "squawk" was a noise that a chicken would make if it had tried to lay a square egg.

Matt understood why he needed to put that number in his transponder. Each plane in the area is assigned a different number; that way the controller who is watching the radar screen can tell which blip is which by the number that appears next to it. Some transponders also tell the controller how high the plane is flying. Matt surely understood how that would help the controllers keep the airplanes separated. And Matt was no dummy; he knew that keeping airplanes separated was a good idea.

Matt called out "Clear!" waited a moment then turned the key. The propeller swung stiffly while the starter turned the flywheel, which moved the crankshaft, which in turn pushed and pulled the pistons up and down until "BOOM," controlled explosions in the combustion chambers made the engine roar to life.

Matt checked the oil pressure gauge to verify that he had oil pressure (which is a really good thing to have). Then he set the throttle to 1000 rpm. Double checking that he had the correct frequency set on his radio, Matt called up Ground Control and told them that he was ready to taxi. "GRAND RAPIDS GROUND, CESSNA 543 DELTA BRAVO AT ZIPPY'S, READY TO TAXI." Less then a moment later a voice answered, "ROGER 3 DELTA BRAVO, TAXI TO RUNWAY 26 LEFT."

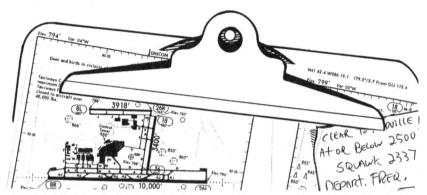

Matt acknowledged the last transmission then proceeded to taxi to runway 26 left. There were quite a few taxiways at this airport, a person could get lost trying to find a runway. Fortunately, Matt had studied the airport diagram the night before and again before he started the engine. With that information, Matt knew how to get to the starting point of runway 26 left.

Glancing down at the runway diagram as he taxied, Matt confirmed that he was heading the right direction. The fact that Ground Control wasn't telling him otherwise meant, to Matt, that he must be doing something right.

Matt stopped short of the runway hold line and performed his pre-flight checklist. When Matt was satisfied that everything was working properly he switched to the tower frequency and told them that he was ready for take-off. "GRAND RAPIDS TOWER, CESSNA 543 DELTA BRAVO READY FOR DEPARTURE, RUNWAY 26 LEFT."

Half a second later the controller answered, "3 DELTA BRAVO, HOLD SHORT FOR AN A-10 ON FINAL."

"3 DELTA BRAVO HOLDING SHORT." Matt acknowledged as looked out to his left to look for the traffic. Out from behind his wing Matt could see a landing light appear followed by a ominous dark mass in the shape of an airplane. Matt didn't argue, you don't win arguments with a 20,000 pound armored aircraft with a 30 millimeter cannon in it's nose. Matt was more than content to sit back and watch one of his favorite airplanes land right there in front of him.

The A-10 that Matt had been waiting for planted it's wheels on the runway for a few seconds then poured on the coals, leaped off the ground again and roared just above the runway building up airspeed as it went. With the landing gear pulled back into the hulk of the aircraft the pilot pulled back on the stick sending that twin turbofanned monster into a super steep climb. To top it off, the Thunderbolt banked steeply to the left and changed to a heading of south before Matt could even blink. Matt had forgotten to breathe while that A-10 went through it's motions. It took a second to remember where he was.

"3 DELTA BRAVO CLEARED FOR TAKEOFF."

Matt acknowledged the tower's call, looked for traffic and taxied on out to the active runway. Pushing in the throttle made that little Cessna's engine roar. Matt had to fight the urge to fly low along the runway and pull up like that A-10.

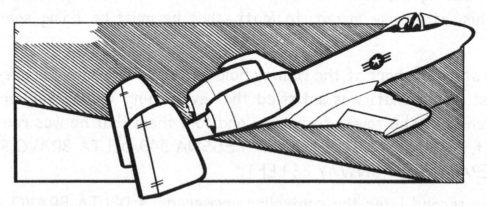

Looking out his back window, Matt made sure that his airplane was still in line with the runway as he climbed up and away from that big airport. Matt knew that he shouldn't drift right or left while departing any airport but this one especially because of the parallel runways; there were planes using 26 right and Matt certainly didn't want to drift into their area.

"3 DELTA BRAVO CONTACT DEPARTURE ON 128.05," the control tower instructed Matt.

"3 DELTA BRAVO SWITCHING TO DEPARTURE 128.05, THANK YOU," Matt twisted the knob on the radio until he had dialed in 128.05, "GRAND RAPIDS DEPARTURE, 3 DELTA BRAVO IS WITH YOU."

Departure Control kept Matt separated from any other traffic as he made his way outbound from the busy airport and onto his next destination.

20 miles out Departure terminated his radar coverage and told Matt to have a good day. Matt was going to miss departure control, he had liked knowing that someone on the ground was looking out for him. Matt had started to enjoy the soothing voice of the controller talking to other pilots and those pilots talking to the controller. It was like listening to talk radio. But now that they were gone, Matt felt kind of alone.

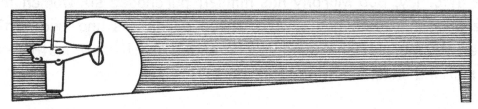

The terrain flowing under Matt on this leg of the trip was a little more rustic. The absence of landmarks below made it hard to check his position. But staying on the calculated heading and using the occasional high tension line, railroad track or small town would be enough to keep Matt from getting lost. When he was satisfied that he knew exactly where he was, he dialed in the frequency for Midville Approach.

Matt listened for a while thinking about what he was planning on saying to the controller. Matt then waited for a break in the radio traffic before he broke in to tell Approach Control that he was heading their way.

The controller that answered seemed extra friendly. Matt felt like he was in good hands as he continued on his flight.

Glancing down occasionally, Matt watched his shadow 2000 feet below him as it traveled over trees and across rivers. It skimmed through a pasture without disturbing a heard of cows. Matt watched his shadow zip through many a backyard giving a split second eclipse to anyone who was looking up.

Meanwhile, down on the ground....

Sam tried to look up at the airplane but it was right in the sun. The sun was much too bright; Sam went back to painting his plywood cut-out cat flat black.

"Maybe I should make a yard shadow of an airplane," Sam thought to himself, "the propeller could spin."

Sam liked that idea. Maybe it would turn into as big a seller as his favorite yard shadow; "Woman with a rolling pin chasing a man."

Sam's attorney; Bob Murphy has himself purchased six women to chase just one poor man. Bob has a wife, three daughters and two mother-in-laws. Even Mr. Murphy isn't sure how he ended up with two mother-in-laws. He only married once; "just his luck," he says.

An hour and a half later, back at the home airport...

Fred had his feet propped up on the desk when he heard the radio call.

"SUMMIT COUNTY UNICOM, CESSNA 543 DELTA BRAVO, EIGHT MILES NORTH, REQUEST AIRPORT ADVISORY."

Picking up the radio's microphone, Fred replied to Matt's request, "3 DELTA BRAVO, SUMMIT COUNTY WINDS ARE FROM THE SOUTHWEST AT 9, NO OTHER REPORTED TRAFFIC."

Fred watched Matt circle and land. It was a bouncy landing but Fred wasn't too surprised, Matt would be very tired after such a long flight. Especially his first solo cross country, Matt's brain would be slightly frazzled. As Fred stepped out onto the porch to meet Matt he looked at his watch, "Well he didn't get lost," Fred thought to himself knowing that Matt would've arrived later if he had gotten lost during the flight.

"Welcome back," Fred shouted to Matt as he walked out towards the plane. Fred could see that Matt was grinning from ear to ear.

After discussing the flight with Fred, Matt tossed his stuff into his car and walked over to the grass next to the hanger and flopped down. It felt good to shut his eyes and relax. He had something in this coat pocket for Spinner too; if the little dog would come out and visit him.

Matt fell asleep before Spinner came bouncing by; keeping his distance of course. The dog's sense of smell told him that the person laying on the grass had food. Spinner liked food. He is able to get plenty of it. There were three different houses plus this airport on his supper route. Spinner had it made. But there was always room for potato chips.

When Matt woke up, there was a dog with potato chip crumbs on his nose curled up asleep next to him. Matt smiled then went back to sleep.

The rain woke Matt up. He was drenched. Matt stood up then wiped the rain out of his eyes. When he looked around he saw that spinner had disappeared; that dog was pretty smart, he had gone somewhere dry.

Matt jumped in his dry car and drove home. "I have some bragging to do," he said very proud of his first solo cross country.

Chapter 6
Final Preparations
(and Flight Test)

Matt completed his last two cross countries in the following week and a half. He enjoyed flying each trip even more than the one before it; Matt was able to enjoy the trips more because he was becoming more comfortable with navigation and communication.

On the last trip, he had gotten up enough nerve to ask permission to go up into the control tower. The controllers were really nice. It helped Matt a lot to see how they did things on their end. They told Matt that he could visit anytime.

With the cross countries out of the way, it was time for review. Matt needed to get ready for his flight test. He would need to fly with Fred and practice just about everything that Fred had taught him so far.

Fred also liked to teach his students how to recover from a spin. Of course, to recover from a spin, you need to get into one.

(dramatic pause)

The stall warning buzzer sounded as Fred continued to pull the yoke clear back into his stomach, the nose of the airplane pointed very steeply skyward. Fred felt the stall and immediately stepped on full left rudder. The left wing dropped, Matt felt that monstrous tingle deep in his gut that always seemed to leave him breathless as the world begun to spin dizzily in front of them.

Fred counted two and a half revolutions then shouted, "opposite rudder," (the ground stopped spinning), "release back pressure," (the airspeed increased and the air started flowing over both wings normally), "pull up". (the plane pulled out of the dive).

As Fred eased the yoke inward and the plane started to level out, Matt felt the force of at least two "G's" pulling him down into his seat.

Matt regained his breath again while Fred initiated a climb up to altitude again; they had lost over one thousand feet in only a few seconds. Matt wanted to do it again.

"Never try any spins on your own," Fred began as they climbed up to 3500 feet again, "Flight instructors are trained extensively in spins and all the different ways you can enter a spin, and of course how to recover from those spins."

It took two days to pry that thrill induced smile off of his face.

"You, my friend are ready to take your flight test." Fred announced to Matt later that week.

Matt had been writing a check to pay for the day's lesson when Fred sprung the news on him.

"Don't look too surprised," Fred stated, "you have shown me that you are a safe and competent pilot who is ready for their flight test."

Laying in bed a couple nights later, Matt had trouble falling asleep. There wasn't any more that Matt could do. Matt had studied hard, practiced hard and Fred had trained him well. So why couldn't he sleep? Just because his flight test was tomorrow was no reason to be worried. Just because he had to fly to a strange airport and convince a Flight Examiner that didn't know Matt from a stranger on the street that he was a knowledgeable and safe pilot capable of hauling an innocent and trusting passenger high up into the sky...

Matt took a deep breath and closed his eyes. His attempt at counting sheep failed when the sheep went from jumping over the fence to flying around doing loops, rolls and other aerial maneuvers

Deciding not to fight in anymore, Matt got up to do some more studying. He sat at his desk and opened one of his books. A few minutes later he fell asleep in his chair.

Arriving at the airport the next morning; the first thing Matt noticed was that the airplane had been pulled out of the hanger and parked nearby. He then saw Fred's silhouette inside the office window taping up a sign that read "GOOD LUCK MATT."

"Very creative," Matt thought to himself as he headed inside to get the keys and to finalize his flight plans.

A little bit later both Fred and Matt walked out of the office. Fred shook Matt's hand and wished him luck. He then turned to go inside. Matt continued his walk out towards the airplane.

"He'll do fine," Fred said to Kristen, the office Manager as he watched Matt pre-flight the airplane, "the test will be tough, but Matt's a good pilot, he'll do fine."

Ten minutes later Matt made his departure call.

"SUMMIT COUNTY TRAFFIC, CESSNA 543 DELTA BRAVO DEPARTING RUNWAY 18."

Fred picked up the office radio's microphone, "HAVE A GOOD FLIGHT 3 DELTA BRAVO."

"Maynerd should be here shortly," Kristen reminded Fred that Matt's friend had signed up for his first lesson today.

Fred zipped out the door and ran to the hanger. He had wanted Piper 6 Romeo Charlie outside and looking good for his new student.

Matt landed at Bluffton Airport about a half hour before his flight test was scheduled to start. He had allowed himself a little bit of extra time to unwind from his flight before jumping right into the test.

After parking and securing the airplane, Matt went inside a building marked "Bluffton Aviation." The fellow behind the counter pointed Matt towards the pilot's lounge. He found the candy machine, made a purchase or two then sat down at a table. Matt was a tad nervous.

Matt checked his watch. He only had a few minutes before his flight test was scheduled to begin. Reluctantly, Matt left the safety and convenience of the candy machine to go out into the main lobby and wait.

"You must be Matt Carr."

The voice had emanated from nowhere, Matt thought as he looked around the room; until the owner of that voice straightened up from behind a counter holding some forms in her hand. "I'm Jessica Wilson, how are you today?"

Matt answered politely as he approached the counter. Matt had been told by an unreliable source that Jessica's nickname was "Dragon Lady Wilson." "She doesn't look like a dragon lady," Matt thought to himself noticing her pleasant smile.

"Come with me and we'll get you started," Mrs. Wilson said as she led

Matt into one of the study rooms. "Fill out these forms here," she handed them to Matt. "When you're done with that let me know and we'll get started on your test." With that Jessica left the room.

After completing the forms and double checking them for a third time, Matt set down his number two pencil, scooted his chair back and stood up. He was as ready as he was going to be. No use putting it off.

It was expected. He had planned on it; but after the second hour of intense questions, trip planning and everything else related to aviation that a private pilot ought to know, Matt sure was ready to move on to something else. It came none to soon when Jessica got up from her chair and asked Matt if he was ready to go flying.

The almost pilot gathered up all of his papers, his plotter and charts and stuffed them neatly into his flight bag. Turning to check that he didn't leave anything behind, Matt left the room and headed for the airplane.

The great outdoors. Matt had worried for weeks about what the weather would have in store for him on this day, the day of his flight test. He had been hoping for a decent day; no 20 knot crosswinds or bad visibility due to haze or anything. The weather was good today. Not perfect but good. Matt imagined that a flight examiner prefers if the weather isn't perfect for a flight test; crosswinds and poor visibility make it more challenging for the applicant.

Jessica Wilson followed Matt around the airplane as he performed the pre-flight inspection. She asked him many questions about what he was checking and why it needed to be checked. Matt answered as best as he could without becoming distracted. (Matt had heard that part of the examiners job was to be distracting; to simulate a talkative passenger).

Satisfied that the airplane was ready, Matt told Mrs. Wilson that the pre-flight inspection was complete. Both she and Matt climbed into the airplane, adjusted their seats and fastened their safety belts.

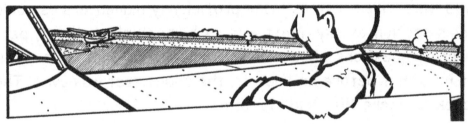

One of the employees of the airport; Carl the line boy, watched as the plane carrying his boss taxied out towards runway 19

"This is my chance to take a little unscheduled break," Carl thought to himself, "Dragon Lady Wilson will be tied up for a while."

Turning for the office, Carl marched his way into the pilot's lounge and parked himself in front of the candy machine.

The candy machine held an overdue surprise for Carl; someone had finally purchased that bag of Billy Chips that had been sitting in the machine since the Carter administration. Finally, that box of Moon Crunchies that Carl has had his eye on wasn't trapped behind a thirty year old bag of chips that no-one would buy.

Dropping in his quarters, Carl pushed the button marked K6 and watched the bag of Moon Crunchies fall into the tray at the bottom of the machine. Carl was in a good mood the whole rest of the day.

It started with a takeoff and ended with a landing; the way that most successful flights ought to be, but the hour and a half in between those two events were filled with as many proficiency maneuvers as could be fit into a given section of sky. Matt was so busy thinking about, performing and answering questions about all the maneuvers that Mrs. Wilson was asking of him, that before he knew it, the flight test was over. They were taxiing back to where they had started.

Matt had dreamt about this moment for a month. All the worrying was done. Matt had done his best to prove that he was a capable pilot. All he had to do now was park the airplane; which he did. After the propeller spun to a stop Matt pulled out the key.

"Congratulations," Mrs. Wilson said after writing something down on her clipboard, "you are now a Private Pilot."

Many things were going through Matt's mind on the flight home. One of which was the Flight Examiner's humbling discussion about how important it is to continue learning and gaining experience. How a pilot should always use common sense, good judgment, and to always take care of their passengers by always flying safely. "Being a pilot is a wonderful privilege," Jessica had said, "but it is also a big responsibility."

Matt wasn't sure if it was the feeling of pride, the excitement of the test or the potato chips that he had munched on earlier, but his stomach felt a little strange.

Matt was tired. It had been a long day already. He was looking forward to a quiet night at home.

"More drinks for everybody," Maynerd shouted to Woody the bartender as he plopped down his empty glass onto the counter with one hand and wiped off his root-beer soda mustache with the other. The sodas were really flowing that night down at Ike's Ice Cream.

Fred, Maynerd and Kristen had conspired this little party in honor of Matt's successes. Matt had figured that something was going on when they all claimed to have car trouble at the same time and how they all needed a ride into town.

It really was a fun time. Everybody from the book was there. People that Matt had never even met before were there toasting him and his new pilot's license. It made him feel good; he had a wonderful time. Matt had worked towards and achieved something that he had always wanted. He will always be proud of what he has just accomplished. His family and friends are also very proud of him; and that is a very good feeling.

The End.

This page
unintentionally
left blank

(I did the "unintentionally left blank" thing on the original books - I thought it was funny - nobody ever mentioned it)
Thanks for reading!

Made in the USA
Coppell, TX
13 December 2024

42319440R00063